All Aboard the
Interstate

Alyxx Meléndez

T0002506

Consultant

Brian Allman
Principal
Upshur County Schools, West Virginia

Publishing Credits

Rachelle Cracchiolo, M.S.Ed., *Publisher*
Emily R. Smith, M.A.Ed., *SVP of Content Development*
Véronique Bos, *VP of Creative*
Dona Herweck Rice, *Senior Content Manager*
Dani Neiley, *Editor*
Fabiola Sepulveda, *Series Graphic Designer*

Image Credits: p10 Art Heritage/Alamy Stock Photo; p11 (top) Library of Congress
[LC-USF34-010815-E]; p11 (bottom) United States Department of Transportation;
p12 (top) Library of Congress [LC-DIG-det-4a27486]; p12 (bottom) Indiana Historic Society;
p13 © SZ Photo/Bridgeman Images; p14 Photo by U.S. Army Signal Corps;
p15 National Archives, Eisenhower Presidential Library, Abilene, Kansas; p17 Los Angeles
Examiner; p19 (top) Library of Congress [Evening star. [volume], July 07, 1961, Page B-2,
Image 24]; p19 (bottom) Courtesy of the Seattle Municipal Archive (image192804);
p22 M&N/Alamy Stock Photo; all other images from iStock and/or Shutterstock

Library of Congress Cataloging-in-Publication Data

Names: Melendez, Alyxx, author.
Title: All aboard the interstate / Alyxx Melendez.
Description: Huntington Beach, CA : TCM, Teacher Created Materials, [2023]
 | Includes index. | Audience: Grades 4-6 | Summary: "The U.S. Interstate
 Highway System gets folks where they need to go. This network of
 fast-paced freeways changed how Americans live and move. The road to the
 Interstate begins with the oldest dirt roads and ends in the future.
 Ride along, and imagine what the next stop might look like"-- Provided
 by publisher.
Identifiers: LCCN 2022021287 (print) | LCCN 2022021288 (ebook) | ISBN
 9781087691091 (paperback) | ISBN 9781087691251 (ebook)
Subjects: LCSH: Interstate Highway System--Juvenile literature. |
 Roads--United States--Juvenile literature.
Classification: LCC HE355 .M45 2023 (print) | LCC HE355 (ebook) | DDC
 388.10973--dc23/eng/20220609
LC record available at https://lccn.loc.gov/2022021287
LC ebook record available at https://lccn.loc.gov/2022021288

Shown on the cover is Houston, Texas.

This book may not be reproduced or distributed in any
way without prior written consent from the publisher.

5482 Argosy Avenue
Huntington Beach, CA 92649
www.tcmpub.com
ISBN 978-1-0876-9109-1

© 2023 Teacher Created Materials, Inc.

Table of Contents

Key West, Florida

United by Highways

Every day in the United States, millions of drivers hop into their vehicles and hit the road. They use **highways** to get to different places. Some drivers might venture only a few miles or kilometers from home. Other drivers might need to pass through two or more states. No matter where they are going, the U.S. **Interstate Highway** System can help them get there.

The U.S. Interstate Highway System is a network of roads. It has 70 main highways and hundreds of shorter roads. They crisscross the country like a giant spiderweb.

There are 46,876 miles (75,440 kilometers) of interstate roads. Every road works the same way, so every mile follows the same rules. Read on to learn these rules, who makes them, and when they might be broken.

What Is a Freeway, Anyway?

Almost all the roads in the U.S. Interstate Highway System are **freeways**. You may have heard people use the words *highway* and *freeway* as if they mean the same thing, but that is not always true. Freeways are a special type of highway with no **intersections**. They have high speed limits because there are no traffic lights or stop signs to slow down traffic. Drivers can count on freeways to take them far and fast.

The Interstate

The whole U.S. Interstate Highway System can be called "the Interstate." Any one interstate highway can also be called "the Interstate." In this case, it is usually the closest interstate highway to the speaker.

Freeways can travel above or below the ground on bridges or in tunnels. All interstate highways are built this way when they need to avoid other roads. On the highways, **on-ramps** allow drivers to join other vehicles. These vehicles might be going very fast. Drivers have to slow down or move to another lane to let cars in. They do not stop on the highway. To **merge** safely, newcomers must catch up! Luckily, on-ramps are usually long enough for drivers to speed up in time. When drivers are ready to exit, **off-ramps** give them a space to slow down. Then, they can stop at an intersection and join slower traffic.

An on-ramp merges onto a highway, while an off-ramp allows vehicles to exit.

highway bridges in Seattle, Washington

toll booths in Florida

Pay to Pass

Toll roads are highways that do not follow a nonstop freeway flow. At some toll booths, traffic comes to a halt, and drivers must pay before they can pass. Some of the first interstate highways were toll roads. At first, states used toll money to finish constructing the interstate system. Today, states use toll money to build new roads and repair old roads. Many toll booths now collect tolls electronically. So, cars no longer have to stop.

Bike Access

Bicycles share the roads with cars even if there is no bike lane available. It is legal to ride a bike on an interstate highway in 11 states. In 5 other states, bikes are allowed on parts of the Interstate. Large, fast vehicles pose a threat to cyclists. Interstate biking is only legal on roads with a small amount of traffic.

Numbers and Signs

Most interstate highways are numbered the same way. Drivers who understand these numbers do not need to rely on maps. Main highways have one- or two-digit numbers. The smaller highways that link them have three-digit numbers. Odd-numbered highways go from north to south. Even-numbered highways go from east to west. But this numbering system is not perfect. Drivers would be confused if interstate highways had the same numbers as other roads. Because of this, interstate numbers are often out of order.

Invisible Interstates

There are 19 unsigned interstate highways. These highways are part of the Interstate, but they are not marked by shields. The longest unsigned interstate highway is I-595 in Maryland. It is 20 miles (32 kilometers) long.

Interstate highways are marked by red and blue shields. The first interstate highways often sped straight through busy cities, leaving travelers with no time to stop and shop. To solve this problem, the states constructed business routes. Business routes are short roads that branch off interstate highways. They are called *loops* or *spurs*, depending on their shapes. Business loops circle back to the highways they came from. Business spurs go straight into a city and do not return to the highway. Business routes are marked by green shields, and they do not need to follow interstate rules.

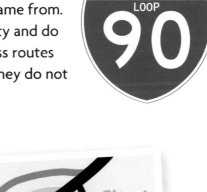

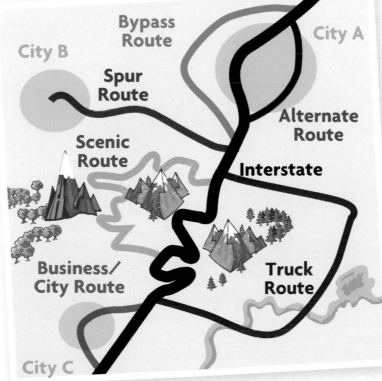

Highway History

Imagine that five friends are taking a road trip together. Each friend drives along the Interstate for eight hours while the others sleep. They could get from Washington, DC, to San Francisco in less than two days. But in 1919, it took future president Dwight D. Eisenhower 62 days to make that trip! Read on to find out why his journey was so hard.

Puppy Power

Most Indigenous peoples from North America did not train animals to help them pull things. But some tribes from the Great Plains trained dogs for this purpose. The dogs carried a vehicle called a **travois**. The travois poles dug deep lines into the edges of the roads. In 1806, Lewis and Clark's famous journey followed travois trails.

Indigenous peoples built the first roads in North America. They built roads thousands of years before the United States came to be. Indigenous roads were dirt paths that followed the curves of the land. European settlers used the same roads when they came to North America in the 1600s. In time, colonists started using horse-drawn carriages. In busy cities, it did not take long for carriage traffic to ruin dirt roads. The horses' hooves dug deep holes in the dirt. Carriage wheels often got stuck in the potholes. The colonists paved over the original roads. They laid gravel and sand on top of the dirt. The paved roads were now strong enough to support horses and carriages. Colonists also built new roads of their own.

Engines are said to have horsepower, like the strength of horses that once did the work.

Workers place gravel on a highway.

Fast and Furious

In 1908, Henry Ford built the Model T, a car like no other. The Model T's top speed was 40 to 45 miles (65 to 70 kilometers) per hour. This was much faster than stagecoaches could travel. Most roads in the United States could not handle such speeds. By the 1920s, Model Ts were common. Ford sold his cars for a cheaper price than any other car. Many families could afford to buy a Model T. They were excited to travel far and fast. But thanks to poor road conditions, cross-country travel was almost impossible. Although paved city streets could handle heavy traffic, most roads in the Midwest were made of dirt. The dirt turned into a muddy mess whenever it rained.

Madam C. J. Walker, a famous businesswoman, drives a Model T in 1912.

street in the 1900s

Usually, the people who lived near roads were in charge of fixing them. People did not have enough money to build better roads, and neither did state governments. The federal government had to help the states. From 1916 to 1952, Congress passed four highway laws. These laws were called Federal-Aid Highway Acts. The acts allowed the federal government to spend some money on roads. But all four acts asked the states to pay for half the cost. The states could not afford this, so construction did not make much progress.

Early EVs

In 1900, about a third of Americans drove electric vehicles, or EVs. Gas-powered cars were loud, smelly, and hard to drive. Many people liked electric cars more. One of these people was Thomas Edison! He helped Henry Ford build EVs. But the Model T changed all that. Model Ts were over $1,000 cheaper than EVs. New technology made gas cars easier to drive.

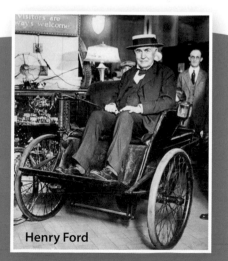

Henry Ford

Ike's Big Idea

In 1919, the U.S. Army sent a group of soldiers and mechanics from Washington, DC, to San Francisco. They traveled in a **convoy** on the Lincoln Highway. They fixed the old road as they drove. One of the soldiers was named Dwight D. Eisenhower. Everyone knew him as "Ike." He wrote all about the 3,200-mile (5,150-kilometer) trip. (Eisenhower would go on to become an important U.S. general and then president.)

Eisenhower and the others had few problems until they reached Nebraska. The western deserts were especially tricky. Sand could be either loose and slippery or cracked and bumpy. Wheels got stuck in ditches, holes, and quicksand. Mountain roads were also rough. The Rockies and Sierra Nevada were full of steep twists and turns. Finally, the convoy hit paved roads in California. They made it to San Francisco. The army's vehicles had broken down 230 times.

The challenges soldiers faced driving on the nation's poor roads inspired highway improvements.

Photo by U.S. Army Signal Corps'

army vehicles on a wide road in Germany

During World War II, the U.S. Army stationed Eisenhower in Germany. He was inspired by Germany's wide, smooth freeways. The German freeway system is called the *autobahn*. Autobahn roads have many lanes, and some parts have no speed limits. Eisenhower dreamed of a day when the United States could have such elegant roads. He was determined to make this dream come true.

The First Tribute to Lincoln

The Lincoln Highway was built in 1913. That is nine years before the Lincoln Memorial was built! After 1956, drivers liked to use the new Interstate (I-80) to get from east to west. New roads buried much of the Lincoln Highway. The old route is marked with statues, signs, and monuments.

A New Dawn

In 1953, Eisenhower was elected president. His new role in the federal government would help him change roads forever. His **administration** spent the next three years planning the Interstate. They drew maps and made rules. Finally, in 1956, Eisenhower showed his plan to Congress. Congress agreed. And so, the Federal-Aid Highway Act of 1956 was signed into law.

The act planned for building 41,000 miles (66,000 kilometers) of road. The states would own all the roads within their borders. But it would be expensive to build these roads and keep them running. Eisenhower knew the states could not pay half the price. State governors did not want to ask people to pay higher taxes. So, the new law only asked the states to pay 10 percent of the costs. Federal funds would cover the other 90 percent. These federal funds came from **excise taxes**. The act placed taxes on cars, trucks, tires, and gas. Anyone who bought these products would pay for a bit of the Interstate.

At first, Congress thought it would cost $27 billion to build the Interstate. Construction was meant to take 10 years. Before long, it became clear that this massive project would cost far more time and money than they thought.

Interstate 10 under construction in Los Angeles, California

Bridge between States

There is one small part of the Interstate that the states did not always own. The Woodrow Wilson Memorial Bridge is one mile (about two kilometers) long. It opened in 1961. One end lies in Virginia. The other end lies in Maryland. The federal government first owned the bridge. Then, it was rebuilt in 2006. Virginia and Maryland both own the new bridge.

Roadblocks

Planning the Interstate was as simple as drawing lines on a map. Building it was a lot more complicated. Some of those lines were drawn straight through areas where people worked and lived. Most of these people were underserved families and people of color. Homes, businesses, parks, and wildlife would be destroyed to make way for concrete. Imagine a family who has lived in their house for many years. Suddenly, someone knocks on their door and says, "The government is building a highway through this house. Please move out." Would the family pack up and leave, or would they fight for their home?

At first, families agreed to move. Government officials offered them money and places to live. But the **displaced** families soon felt like they had not gotten fair deals. Money could not buy back their lands, and government housing could not replace their homes. In the 1960s and 1970s, all over the nation, people protested against freeways. These people were **activists**. They asked their neighbors to help protest against the Interstate. When the activists formed a large group, their voices grew loud. Politicians heard them. Many freeway **revolts** convinced the government to stop construction.

Who Was First?

Missouri and Kansas both claim to have had the first interstate highway. It is hard to say which state is correct. I-70 in Missouri was the first interstate highway to *begin* construction. I-70 in Kansas was the first to *finish*. The Kansas road was already being built when the 1956 Act passed. Interstate funds paid for the rest of the highway.

KEY TO OTHER ROADS
Hearing Set on Vital Mile

Several highly-disputed interstate projects hinge on the outcome of a hearing to be held tomorrow for a vital one-mile stretch of freeway in Arlington County.

The hearing will be for a link between Interstate 66 and the proposed Three Sisters Bridge. The link is to be called Interstate 266, and will be built in Spout Run Park.

This is the only hearing required by law before the State Highway Commission can approve the project and submit it for Federal approval. The hearing starts at 10:30 a.m. at Arlington Courthouse.

D. C. Controversy

Civic groups already have opposed the Three Sisters Bridge. The groups argue that its completion would demand construction of a freeway through Glover-Archbald Park.

The National Capital Plan-

GEO. WASH. MEM. PARKWAY

LORCOM LANE

24th ST. N.

POTOMAC

THREE SISTERS BRIDGE

SPOUT RUN PARKWAY

INTERSTAT

Heavy line shows propos and controversial ram Three Sisters Bridge.

Fight Urged On Freeway For McLean

A meeting to protest a freeway proposed for the McLean area drew more than 350 citizens to Chesterbrook School last night.

David N. Yerkes of 4311 Kirby road, McLean, a Washington architect, organized the gathering to oppose an express highway sought by Fairfax planners for the Little Pimmitt Run Valley.

Speakers argued that the freeway was not needed and that it would lower property values.

The route, one of eight considered by the Fairfax Planning Commission, would connect the Dulles Airport freeway and a proposed bridge to the District at Arizona avenue N.W. An estimated 60 to 100 homes would have to be destroyed if the route is approved.

freeway under construction through Chinatown, Seattle, 1966

19

Congress did not realize the Interstate would cost so much money. This is partly because they did not calculate the cost of **feeder roads**. To be an Interstate, highways need good feeder roads. Cars have to cruise smoothly onto and off highways. In the end, the Interstate cost nearly $129 billion. The federal government paid more than $114 billion of that cost. But remember the excise taxes on gas and tires? People who drive often will buy more gas and wear down their cars and tires faster. That means that people who use highways more often will also pay more to repair them.

Results

Thanks to the Interstate, vehicles could cross the country in record time. Fast transit improved people's lives in many ways. Grocery stores could sell foods from faraway states. Drugstores could sell medicine fast enough to save lives. And people could explore the nation more freely. But interstate highways often replaced the roads that had come before them. Famous highways such as U.S. Route 66 were no longer popular. The stores and motels along old highways shut down one by one. Tourist attractions turned into ghost towns. Interstate highways both shaped and disrupted the flow of American life.

Border to Border

Only one interstate highway in the United States can take you directly from the Canadian border to the Mexican border. It is I-5 on the West Coast. It stretches from northern Washington to San Diego, California.

original section of Route 66, completed in 1931

Down the Road

The 1956 Federal-Aid Highway Act was not the last highway act. There would be two more acts with the same name. The 1968 Act built new highways. The Interstate grew by 1,500 miles (about 2,400 kilometers). This act also helped displaced people find places to live. The 1973 Act built more feeder roads. It also changed how federal funds could be spent. Now, states could spend Interstate money on public transit as well as roads. Both acts paid for new road-safety programs.

In 1982, lawmakers decided to shake up their acts with fresh new names. This started with the Surface Transportation Assistance Act (STAA). The STAA taxed people five cents more for every gallon of gas they bought. Next came the Transportation Equity Act (TEA). These acts passed in 1998 and 2005. The TEA set new rules for

Bus travelers stop in Utah, 1955.

road planning. New roads had to be fast and safe. They had to help the economy and the environment. They also had to connect smoothly and not just to other roads. Trains, planes, and ships were included in the TEA's plan. This would speed up transportation for **freight** as well as people.

Interstate 80, Utah

Coast to Coast

Three interstate highways reach from coast to coast. They are I-10, I-80, and I-90. Drivers can visit the Atlantic Ocean and the Pacific Ocean just a few days apart. This journey could prove which coast has the sunniest beaches or the best-tasting seafood!

There are more than 4 million miles (6.5 million kilometers) of roads in the United States. That still is not enough for the nonstop modern world. Twenty percent of those roads are in poor condition. Drivers need more lanes and better highways. Once again, states need federal funds to pay for them.

The 2015 FAST Act is a modern highway law. FAST stands for Fixing America's Surface Transportation. President Barack Obama signed it into law. The law allowed the government to spend billions on transportation. The highway budget was about $165 billion under the FAST Act. The FAST Act expired in 2021. It will be up to the federal government to come up with future plans for maintaining the nation's highways.

Hawai'i, Alaska, and Puerto Rico

Cars cannot drive to the **contiguous** United States from Hawai'i or Puerto Rico. But the U.S. Interstate Highway System still pays for some roads there and in Alaska. These roads do not have to follow the same rules as other interstates. Red and blue shields mark the three "interstates" in Hawai'i. Alaska and Puerto Rico each have four "interstates." None of those eight highways use interstate shields or numbers.

What Is Next?

New construction will be expensive, and traffic will slow down for months. But **visionaries** believe that this is not a problem. Early road projects proved that short delays lead to speed in the long run. And when the government pays for a large project, thousands of workers get new jobs. Construction workers, city planners, and scientists from many fields are all part of building good highways. Workers who improve the Interstate will be paid today to keep tomorrow moving.

Transportation Today

The Interstate was once the dream of American drivers. After more than half a century, it may be time to go back to the dreaming board. The world's population grows, and humans are learning how to travel faster. More drivers create more traffic, and more traffic creates more problems.

highway in New York

The freeways of tomorrow must have more lanes to fit more traffic. But construction can also harm the environment. Roads are often built where animals live. Also, car crashes kill a million animals in the United States each day. Wildlife bridges can reduce that grim number. Animals can safely cross freeways over these dirt-covered bridges. This is just one **innovative** way to build highways that respect Earth. Scientists are improving clean energy technology each day. Perhaps Interstate highways can change with the times.

land bridge for animal crossings over a highway

Just as in times past, *anyone* can make a change happen. To create a new Interstate, just make sure the design follows all the right laws. Then, send it to your state transportation department. After that, the rest might just be history!

Tolls Today

At first, toll booths were installed on the Interstate to pay for the rest of the road. Even though the full cost of Interstate construction was paid long ago, toll booths still collect payments. Heavy traffic is hard on roads, so there is always a project for tolls to fund. Today, states use these funds to maintain all their roads.

Map It!

The U.S. Interstate Highway System offers many routes between and among the 48 continguous states. Travelers need to use maps, apps, or the internet to decide the best way to reach their destinations.

For this activity, use a map of the Interstate to plan your perfect road trip.

1. Form a group with two to four friends or classmates.
2. Each member should choose a state that seems great to visit and can be reached by interstate from another state. No two people should pick the same state.
3. Shade or color each of these states on the map.
4. As a group, discuss routes the trip could follow, connecting each of these states. Trace routes with pencil.
5. Decide which route would be best to take. Think about the length of the route, sights along the way, and travel challenges. Trace the chosen route with marker, and erase the other routes.
6. Write a travel plan on another sheet of paper. Include the number of each highway in the order decided by the group. Make sure to include the direction of each highway. For example, I-5 North to I-80 East.

All Aboard the
Interstate

Alyxx Meléndez

Gateway Arch, St. Louis

Kansas City barbecue

Garden of the Gods, Colorado Springs

Nashville to
Colorado Springs
24 West
to 57 North
to 70 West
to Kansas City
Continue 70 West
to 25 South
to Colorado Springs
to Garden of the Gods
State Park

Glossary

activists—people who take strong action to make changes in politics or society

administration—group of people who work under a certain president

contiguous—being in actual contact; referring to 48 U.S. states (excluding Alaska and Hawai'i)

convoy—a group of vehicles traveling together, often military

displaced—removed from an area, usually by force

excise taxes—taxes on certain goods that fund projects related to those goods

feeder roads—roads leading onto and off of a highway

freeways—fast-moving highways that do not cross other roads

freight—goods that are moved in large amounts

highways—main roads that pass through more than one city

innovative—having new ideas

intersections—areas where roads cross and traffic is controlled by lights or signs

interstate highway—a highway that connects states

merge—drive from one lane to another

off-ramps—short roads that lead cars off of a highway

on-ramps—short roads that lead cars onto a highway

revolts—organized protests against something unfair

travois—woven basket tied between two long poles, used to drag goods

visionaries—people who learn from the past to imagine a better future

Index

Traffic in the 1960s fills a freeway in Los Angeles, California.

Learn More!

Dwight Eisenhower was not the first person with high hopes for highways. Many brilliant minds helped map out the roads that later became interstate highways. Just a few of these people are Woodrow Wilson, Thomas Harris MacDonald, and John J. Pershing.

✳ Choose one of these three people, and create a poster about their contributions to U.S. highways.

✳ On a small part of the poster, write a few facts about that person's life.

✳ On the largest part of the poster, answer the following questions:

- What was the name of this person's plan to improve the U.S. highway system?

- In what year did they create their plan?

- What organization did they work for at that time?

- How did their work pave the way for the Interstate?